AT SCHOOL

Written By E.C. Andrews

Letters from Around the World

KidHaven PUBLISHING

Published in 2025 by
KidHaven Publishing, an Imprint of
Greenhaven Publishing, LLC
2544 Clinton St., Buffalo, NY 14224

Written by: E.C. Andrews
Edited by: Elise Carraway
Designed by: Amelia Harris

Cataloging-in-Publication Data

Names: Andrews, E.C.
Title: At school / E.C. Andrews.
Description: Buffalo, New York : KidHaven Publishing, 2025. | Series: Letters from around the world | Includes glossary and index.
Identifiers: ISBN 9781534546950 (pbk.) | ISBN 9781534546967 (library bound) | ISBN 9781534546974 (ebook)
Subjects: LCSH: Schools--Juvenile literature.
Classification: LCC LB1513.A534 2025 | DDC 371.01--dc23

Manufactured in the United States of America

CPSIA compliance information: Batch #CSKH25
For further information contact Greenhaven Publishing LLC at 1-844-317-7404.

Please visit our website, www.greenhavenpublishing.com.
For a free color catalog of all our high-quality books, call toll free 1-844-317-7404 or fax 1-844-317-7405.

Find us on

Image Credits

All images are courtesy of Shutterstock.com, unless otherwise specified. With thanks to Getty Images, Thinkstock Photo, and iStockphoto. Cover images – NataLT, Akane1988, estherpoon, Fourleaflover, Puwadol Jaturawutthichai, Tartila, The img, Colorfuel Studio, Jeppe Gustafsson, Ground Picture. Recurring images – KanKhem, Olga_C. 2 – ina9, ESB Professional. 4–5 – Colorfuel Studio. 6–7 – NIKCOA, Neliakott, svekolka, OlgaChernyak, Elena Chevalier, Monkey Business Images. 8–9 – CECIL BO DZWOWA, Colorfuel Studio, SofiaV, Igdeeva Alena. 10–11 – jianbing Lee, sweettoiletpaper, LP2 Studio, Illerlok_xolms, h0lyland. 12–13 – Fernanda_Reyes, Tartila. 14–15 – Irina Wilhauk, juninatt, Jeppe Gustafsson, Mind Pixell, kelttt, Daisy and Bumble. 16–17 – ANURAK PONGPATIMET, milatas, Portrait Image Asia, Raura7, hvostik. 18–19 – J.P. Junior Pereira, StockSmartStart. 20–21 – Ground Picture, WESTOCK PRODUCTIONS, Mohammad Shahnawaz, PCH.Vector. 22–23 – ESB Professional, Janis Abolins, Pressmaster, Shchus, Colorfuel Studio.

CONTENTS

Words that look like this can be found in the glossary on page 24.

LETTERS FROM EVERYWHERE

Hello! I am Samantha. I live in the U.S., but I have lots of pen pals from around the world. We write to each other to share what life is like in our countries.

I told my pen pals that every morning, I say the U.S. Pledge of Allegiance with my class. My pen pals all have different school traditions. Let me share their letters with you!

Pen pals are friends you talk to by writing letters!

A LETTER FROM FRANCE

Salut! My name is Camille. I go to school in France. In my country, food is very important. We have a two-hour lunch break to eat and play.

In France, schools serve four-course meals. They come with dessert!

Today is Wednesday. Wednesdays are my favorite days because our lessons finish at lunchtime and I get to go to art club after school. I get to paint with my friends. I love learning about art.

A LETTER FROM ZIMBABWE

I am Anopa. This is my school in Zimbabwe. Some of my friends ride bikes to school because they live far away, but I like to walk. We have one teacher who teaches all our subjects.

At my school, we study Shona. Shona is one of Zimbabwe's official languages. It is spoken in a lot of places. My friend's school teaches a Zimbabwean language called Ndebele instead.

P.S. Most schoolchildren in Zimbabwe wear uniforms. Do you have a uniform?

A LETTER FROM CHINA

My name is Hong Lu. I go to school in China. We have to do one hour of exercise every morning. It wakes me up and gets me ready for lessons!

Our lessons end later than a lot of other schools, but we get a longer lunch break. During lunch, we can sometimes take a nap if we want to.

A LETTER FROM MEXICO

Hola! My name is Elena. In my country, Mexico, we start school early and finish at lunchtime. I like to go home for lunch and have a siesta during the hottest part of the day.

P.S. Mexico can get hot. Siestas help us rest and stay cool.

Sometimes, I go to afternoon classes. I like the extra classes because they help me with subjects that I struggle with. I find math quite hard, but my extra classes help me understand it more.

A LETTER FROM SWEDEN

My name is Ebba. I go to school in Sweden. It snows a lot in my country. Our outdoor shoes can get very wet, so we take our outdoor shoes off before going into the classroom.

We are not allowed to wear outdoor coats in the classroom either. But it can get very cold in the winter. I like to wear lots of wool sweaters and warm socks.

A LETTER FROM JAPAN

My name is Sakura. I go to school in Japan. When we start school, we each get a backpack from our families called a randoseru. We keep it until we finish primary school.

This is what my randoseru looks like.

I get the train to school on my own. At the end of the day, we all help to clean the school before we leave. We then take after-school classes at a juku.

A LETTER FROM BRAZIL

My name is Bruna. I go to school in Brazil. I like learning languages at school. We study English, Spanish, and Portuguese. A lot of children go to school in Brazil.

Some of us go to school at different times so there are not too many people in the classroom. I go to school in the morning. My brother goes to school in the afternoon.

A LETTER FROM INDIA

Hello! My name is Pavitr. I come from India. In school, we learn Hindi and English. They are both official languages in India. Hindi is my favorite subject!

What languages do you learn at your school?

When we eat lunch, we sit on mats on the floor. Sitting on the floor to eat is normal here.

I do not get any homework, so I do not have to carry any heavy books home.

EVERYWHERE IS DIFFERENT

School can be very different all around the world. My pen pals' schools all have their own way of doing things that are unique to their country. I love to learn about how other children live.

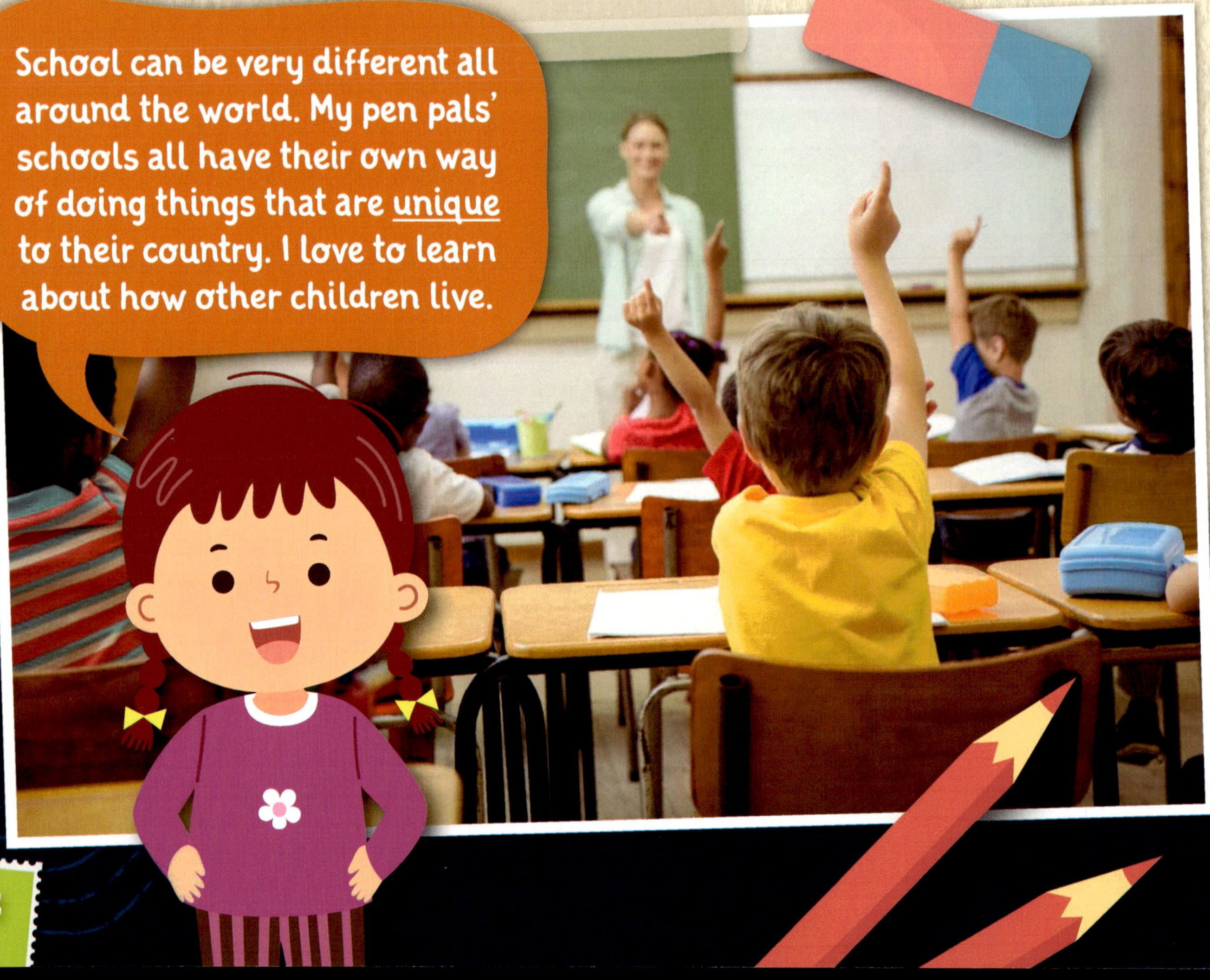

I bet there are things about your school that other children would find surprising. Is there something interesting about your school? Why not write to me about it? I would love to be your pen pal!

GLOSSARY

four-course	made up of or served in four parts
hola	Spanish word for "hello"
juku	evening schools in Japan
official languages	the languages used in a country that have been chosen by the government and are taught in school
salut	French word for "hi"
siesta	Spanish word for an afternoon nap
subjects	topics that are taught in class
traditions	practices that have been done for a long time
unique	unlike anything or anyone else
U.S. Pledge of Allegiance	a sentence that is said in the United States as a way of showing respect to the country

INDEX